Manipulation

----- ✥✥✥✥ -----

*The Definitive Guide to Understanding
Manipulation, Mind Control and NLP*

Table of Contents

Introduction 1

Chapter 1: What is Manipulation and How does it Work? 3

Chapter 2: The Benefits of Learning about this Skill 13

Chapter 3: Manipulation and Influence Techniques 19

Chapter 4: How to Recognize Negative Manipulation 23

Chapter 5: How to Avoid being Manipulated 29

Chapter 6: A Guide to Positive Manipulation (Persuasion) ... 39

Conclusion 49

Introduction

I want to thank you and congratulate you for downloading the book, *"Manipulation: The Defining Guide to Understanding Manipulation, Mind Control, and NLP"*.

There are always instances, throughout life, where you can't get exactly what you desire, but you never need to settle for being disappointed. Instead, you can learn about manipulation and mind control, how to use it on others with NLP techniques, and spot when others are using it on you. Most people believe that manipulation is a negative thing, and the concept generally gets a bad rap, but that all depends on what type of manipulation you're using. In this book, we will go over the following:

- **Defining Manipulation:** As mentioned above, there is a lot of misunderstanding surrounding this word, what it means, how it's used, and more. In this guide, you will learn what you need to know about the concept of manipulation and general persuasion and influence.

- **The Benefits of Using it Right, and How to do that:** Manipulation can be used in a positive way that benefits all parties involved, but this is something you have to learn about to master.

- **How to Spot and Avoid Negative Manipulation:** If you aren't aware of what it looks like to be manipulated by others, it's almost certain that it will happen to you, which could be dangerous. Leaving

Introduction

yourself upon to the whim of whoever wishes to manipulate you could have long lasting harmful effects

Thanks again for downloading this book, I hope you enjoy it!

Chapter 1:

What is Manipulation and How does it Work?

Manipulation exists in everyone's life on the planet. Within the human mind, a few different groups of shortcuts exist that leave us vulnerable to manipulation, and there are countless combinations and variations of these. Many people are even willing to put their lives on the line for them, which is no exaggeration. Some people will pick a job they hate, drink poison, or risk their lives in war. They might even get into an accident on the street completely unaware that they are following through actions of a story they read in the paper the day before. Most importantly, they would be spending money and time.

What is Manipulation?

Manipulation is the influence a person uses to try to alter the perceptions or behaviors of others. Often, it's done through underhanded, deceptive, or abusive techniques, but not always. In some people's opinions, when a manipulator advances their own interests using these techniques, without consideration for the needs of others, the methods are exploitative.

What is Manipulation and How does it Work?

- **Negative Manipulation:** This is when you intentionally withhold information from someone to get what you want, play up your own emotions in a false way to persuade someone, or otherwise threaten them indirectly for selfish reasons. Negative manipulation has harmed countless people in the world. Being under the negative manipulation of another person can make you feel like you're crazy, or act in ways that you would normally never act. We will cover this in more detail in later chapters.

- This method of manipulation relies on hidden agendas, ulterior motives, and attempts to force others to give into your will. Although the manipulator looks in control and strong on the surface, they often feel very insecure on the inside; otherwise they wouldn't need to engage in such behaviors. The actions of these people (such as disregarding and exploiting the rights of other people) are a signal of a lack of health, on a mental level. In fact, people who engage in these behaviors have a hard time finding and keeping positive relationships with others.

- **Positive (or Ethical) Manipulation:** Also known as persuasion or influence, this is when you convince someone to come around to your ways of thinking or acting, but in a way that also benefits them. This has a positive, rather than harmful, effect. There are a few clear distinctions between negative and positive manipulation, and it's important to make sure you know the difference. Everyone uses positive manipulation and influence to further our own goals with other people, which is perfectly fine and normal. This method of manipulation acknowledges the boundaries and rights of others, and uses honest and direct communication.

- This method of manipulation is a simple way to function efficiently and effectively in your environment, and to benefit and make use of the social order that exists in our world. It recognizes that other people have a basic integrity, and a choice of whether or not to follow through with your persuasion attempts. In essence, this acknowledges that each person should be autonomous and acknowledges a baseline of human respect between you and others. We are all social creatures who need each other, in one way or another.

What is NLP and How does it Relate to this?

NLP (or Neuro-Linguistic Programming) is a study that focuses on the elements that allow us to experience the world. These elements are programming, language, and the neurology of our brains. Our neurological systems control the way our physical bodies work, language regulates the way we communicate with the world and other people, and the programming we go through in life decides what our models of reality will look like. All of this determines who we will be, what we will think like, what our habits will be, and what type of lives we will lead. We will discuss, in more detail, NLP techniques in a later chapter of this book.

Being aware of these definitions allows you to use knowledge to better your life. When you are aware of what methods can be used to influence you, suddenly you are empowered to make choices about what does. This book will teach you how to recognize manipulation methods being used today, along with methods for resisting them. You will also learn about using the ingrained mental shortcuts we all have to persuade,

What is Manipulation and How does it Work?

manipulate, and influence others. Let's look at something we are all familiar with, advertising, to illustrate how this works.

Manipulation in Advertising vs. Personal Manipulation:

How exactly is manipulation in advertising done? Advertisers utilize many different techniques for manipulating customers or potential consumers. These include appeals to emotions and feelings, ads that are disguised as other forms of entertainment, and ads that appeal to insecurities or fears. As these strategies become more and more sophisticated and complex, consumers can recognize and resist the manipulative or deceptive tactics by learning more about how they work. In addition to this, you can apply this knowledge the techniques that people use to manipulate each other. Let's look at some of the manipulation techniques of advertising, to get a better understanding of this subject:

- **Emotional Reactions:** Advertisers know that emotions are a great way to elicit specific feelings in people, and they use this to their advantage. Advertisers often play up or emphasize the feelings that products will bring you, rather than actual characteristics or qualities of the products. In fact, a lot of ads aim to elicit a feeling response that distracts customers from considering the functionality or value of the product. They might show specific scenarios that consumers can remember or relate to in some other way, like your first child's birth, or a date. This increases the feeling response and engagement, emotionally, that viewers will feel with that product.

Manipulation

- This same technique is used in interpersonal manipulation. For example, a friend or significant other who is trying to convince you to do something you don't want to do might try to encourage you by telling you it will be fun, or even bringing up past memories to elicit a feeling response in you. Some may also use fear tactics to elicit a negative emotion, or a fear of a negative emotion in others to get them to do what they want. This is, for example, used often by parents who threaten their children with being punished unless they follow through on orders.

- **Ads Disguised as Simple Entertainment:** It becomes more and more common that ads disguise themselves as simple entertainment, providing depictions of humorous or relatable narratives to attract consumers. Skillful or clever screen writing, cute animal mascots, and unique or memorable strategies all help to make customers feel more engaged, and thus likelier to remember the product being advertised. Some ads will even show the most outrageous scenarios they can invent to make this happen. Companies that sell products that are unhealthy, like candy or beer, tend to utilize humor techniques to distract viewers from detrimental or negative factors of products.

- This type of technique used in advertising can be compared to interpersonal manipulation tactics which misrepresent true intentions. For example. Someone who is manipulating you might tell you that their intentions are something completely different than they really are. They might pretend to only wish to entertain or please you, when they truly have ulterior motives.

What is Manipulation and How does it Work?

They might also use flattery or other false narratives to further their own personal agenda.

- **Using Fear and Insecurity:** Advertisers are famous for preying on the insecurities of consumers. For example, TV commercials may depict a character that they wish to portray as "unattractive" or lesser than others by focusing on a particular "flaw", such as baldness, or yellowing teeth. They then appear to offer the magical solution to the problem by attempting to sell you their product. Another example of using fear as an ad tactic is advertising for soap or other cleaning products during times when sickness is prevalent. Many times, their products don't actually help combat the sickness at all.

- An example of this tactic being used in interpersonal relations is in romantic relationships. Perhaps one person is ready to break up and move on, but the other is afraid to live without them. Instead of respecting the person's choice to leave and move on with their life, they try to appeal to that person's insecurities by insinuating that they will never find someone as good. Fear is a perfect example of a negative manipulation tactic that is good to guard yourself against. We will show you how to do that later on in the book.

The Rule of Reciprocation, a Common Technique:

One common and famous technique for manipulating others using automatic or subconscious behavior, is called the rule of reciprocation. The basic idea behind this "rule" is that if someone else does something nice for you, you should do something for them in return. This is something we are all taught from childhood, either directly or indirectly, and is so ingrained that nearly nobody questions it. This tactic is used often to manipulate others.

- **Sample Counters:** Think about samples given out at grocery stores. The idea behind them is that if someone gives you a taste of something at no cost, your mind will see it as a favor and make you more likely to purchase their product. Instead of having people paid to walk around and ask people if they would like to buy something, they have people giving out free stuff, which makes others more obligated to listen to what the sales person has to say.

- **Door to Door Fundraisers:** Another area this tactic is used in is fundraising efforts. When someone goes door to door to try to collect donations from people, they are a lot more likely to get someone to listen to what they have to say (and therefore, at times, donate) if they offer something first. Simple techniques like this can make donations multiply and sky rocket, due to basic psychology manipulation techniques.

This rule applies to favors big and small and you don't necessarily feel obligated to return the same amount of "good" or favor back to someone who has done something for you. In fact, you can do someone a tiny favor, and then ask them for something big, and the trick still has an effect. For example, you could offer to help someone carry groceries in from their car, or mention that you have dedicated hours of your life to them (implying that they now owe you big.) Of course, this type of manipulation can be used for good aims, such as getting your child to do their schoolwork or study for a test, convincing your sick mother to go to the doctor, or getting your manager to give you a raise. These techniques can be used to discover the true reason behind issues going on at

What is Manipulation and How does it Work?

work or in the family, and help people move past harmful habits they are stuck in.

Ways of using these Techniques in Everyday Life:

There are important distinctions between NLP methods and the techniques listed above. A quality NLP method benefits people and incorporates mental tricks like the one mentioned above (reciprocity). However, you don't have to be aware of NLP or hypnosis methods to use manipulation techniques.

- **The Hypnotist Metaphor:** You might find it useful to think about the following metaphor. Envision being a hypnotist who must convince a patient or subject to stop moving and be completely still. You have to get them to look forward and ignore all noises besides your instructions. You could use techniques for building rapport, or trance techniques, which may or may not actually work.

- **Considering the Person:** It's important, when learning about or trying to partake in manipulation, to know your subject. If the person you are trying to get to focus, for example, has been employed by the military at one point, wearing official general clothes from their army and calling out "Attention!" will do the trick. Conditioning is something that is often with us for life, whether we are aware of it or not. This means that you are not creating new responses or reactions in the person, but simply calling upon something that already exists within them.

Manipulation

How are Mental Shortcuts related to Manipulation?

It's obvious why these behaviors are thought of as automatic reactions, but how are mental shortcuts related? In the language of NLP, this could be called distortion, deletion, or generalization, but we are going to keep it simple for now. Let's start with how human beings think and relate to the world, something everyone has firsthand experience with.

- **Shortcuts for Survival:** Our world is complicated and we are constantly surrounded by new stimuli. It's impossible for humans to constantly think about every factor that is needed, which is why certain processes are automated. Perhaps we would still survive without this, but it would be extremely inefficient. Think, for example, about operating your car. Can you recall when you first started driving, and the way you needed to pay close attention to every single part of the process? But now, it's simply automatic. This is done by utilizing mental shortcuts.

- Rather than having to stop and agonizingly consider every angle of every sign or light, you already know what to do instinctively due to repetition. Think now about reading information or news on the internet. How do you figure out whether stories you're reading are true or false? You aren't going to thoroughly research every article every time. Instead, you apply mental shortcuts to find your answer and opinion.

- **How these Shortcuts leave us Vulnerable:** This part is important. Not everyone realizes that they are employing these mental shortcuts throughout the day. They simply happen automatically, without much thought, after all that's the point of them, right? But

What is Manipulation and How does it Work?

this automated process of thinking and acting can leave us vulnerable to others who wish to manipulate these tendencies. Although we need these automatic processes and shortcuts for survival, to make decisions quickly with minimal thought and effort, they are often used against us.

- The examples above given of advertising manipulation tactics are a depiction of this at work, as are the tactics used by politicians during speeches. Everyone knows the terms "clearance" and "sale." When signs exclaiming either one of these are placed out front of a store, people know to expect good deals and bargains on their shopping trips. When we see an advert claiming that there is a limited time, great offer happening at their location, our subconscious minds pick up on this.

These mental shortcuts are all around us and a very important part of our lives. Statistics prove that a guy who is better looking will receive a less harsh conviction or sentence in court. Studies have shown that American citizens are far more likely to vote for someone who looks friendly and paternal, because of our mental associations of seeing people like this as more trustworthy. Salespeople will be more successful in their sales if they simply present their items in a certain way. We cannot control our own automatic thought processes and conditioning, but becoming aware of this is beneficial for many reasons.

Chapter 2:

The Benefits of Learning about this Skill

Learning about manipulation, both in its positive and negative forms, is important for any human who wishes to function in a healthy way. Using persuasion techniques from NLP studies can increase your ability to ethically manipulate others and be more influential, in general. Ethical manipulation is an important skill in life, and can be used for influencing clients, members of your family, or colleagues at work. Anyone who learns about NLP for this reason will access useful and powerful abilities to help support the process of ethical manipulation and persuasion.

The Benefits of Knowing about Persuasion and Manipulation:

Mastering these skills and the fine art of ethical manipulation will give you new opportunities for increases in your sales numbers, getting to know important or influential figures, better self-esteem, and the ability to express yourself naturally and authentically. The art of persuasion is an important part of the theory of communication, and these methods help create and foster healthy relations on a community level, along with customer and employee relations. When you are good at employing the correct use of argumentation, it will lead to

The Benefits of Learning about this Skill

raises, promotions, and influential or powerful positions. Let's look at a few more benefits to this:

- **Rapport:** One important benefit to learning about ethical manipulation is using it to build rapport with others. Rapport is what helps us feel at ease with another person, feel common ground, and look for qualities shared in common. It is necessary for all positive interactions and achieving goals that include other people. Essentially, this happens when you feel comfortable with someone, relate to them easily, and have a warm interaction with them. Rapport relies on seeing common ground between you and another person.

- It's an important aspect of persuasion and manipulation because people are a lot more likely to do favors for others, or simply agree with them, if they see that person as similar to themselves. Therefore, everyone who knows how to ethically persuade others is aware of building rapport. In this book, we will give you a few methods for doing this with many different types of people. No matter how different the person seems from you, it's possible to find common ground and build rapport if you simply know how.

- **Seeing the Needs and Wants of Others:** When you are effective at persuading other people, or knowing how to read signs of them trying to persuade, you catch a glimpse into what they find the most important. In this way, you can understand humanity on a deeper level, and use this information to get ahead in life. When you recognize others' wants and needs, not only do you better understand them as an individual, but

Manipulation

you can become closer. This is what separates positive and negative manipulation.

- **Effective Communication:** Rapport-building and recognizing the needs of others are foundations that can lead to effective communication. Effectively communicating is useful for countless reasons, among which are conflict resolution, getting ahead in your career, and resolving conflicts on a professional and personal level. Let's look at the example of building healthy relations with employees from your work. Talking to them about benefit decreases, or impending layoffs, along with other unpleasant company decisions, requires a certain level of savvy that can be gained using ethical manipulation techniques.

- One method for dong this relies on reaching your listeners using logic and facts. You could, for example, show that if your business doesn't close down a certain property, the rest of your businesses will have to close down. The second method relies on the fact that your listeners are paying attention mostly on an emotional plane, rather than using logic. In situations like this, appealing to empathy by illustrating examples of families who will suffer as a result of not taking action is more effective. As mentioned earlier in the book, knowing your audience is important for effectively persuading people.

- **Finding Shared Values with Anyone:** There are times, in life, when we are forced to work along with or spend time with people who seem very different from us. When you are effective at persuasion and ethical manipulation, this becomes easy. You can simply find shared values with them, no matter how different they appear to be on the surface. This allows you access to the skills of lightening tension in tough situations, or getting people to do you favors readily. People are more likely to help those who they see as similar to them, meaning that knowing how to find similarities is a must for interpersonal relations.

- **Beating Resistance:** Marketing depends entirely on the buying habits of consumers. One hard habit to beat is buyer resistance in consumers. Effectively persuading buyers means helping them to feel at ease with their choices, while simultaneously improving your sales numbers. A main factor in doing this is displaying to the buyer your understanding of the hard choice they are facing. Letting them know that you are aware of how difficult the purchase is and understand their feelings can allow them to let down their guard.

- This allows the buyer to see you more as a human. They may then make a purchase that benefits them and you, as the sales person. This of course applies not just to sales, but to interpersonal situations. Empathizing with another person is a great way to get them to open up, feel more comfortable, and become decisive about important choices.

- **Expressing Yourself more Effectively:** Skills in influence and positive manipulation helps individuals to express themselves authentically. Constructing logical and sound arguments that people come to agree with creates and sustains self-assuredness and confidence. Arguments that use logic rely on facts, not just opinions. Even though a person might start with a certain idea or opinion, researching the situation or material will allow them a chance to give others important and valid data and information. Speakers who are truly powerful and influential use facts to support their arguments, and use that information to prove that they are correct.

Techniques for Persuasion and Manipulation Skills:

This book will go over many different techniques for this, but let's start with the following basics:

- **Mirroring:** This is one of the quickest ways to build rapport with someone you just met. You pay attention to their bodily movements, tone of voice, and values, and mirror them subtly. For example, if someone is standing with their arms crossed, do the same thing. If they are speaking excitedly and quickly, match their tone and pitch. This must be done in a very subtle way or it will have the opposite effect you're hoping for. The reason why this is so effective is because you can eventually have someone follow you to a conclusion or decision that you wish for them to reach.

- **Questioning:** Another technique for this is discovering what people need and want by asking questions. You do this to elicit their personal values and figure out what they think is most important in this world, then you can appeal to those values by aligning your idea, service, or product with what they find important.

- **Honesty:** This is a key difference in ethical manipulation and negative, selfish manipulation. Effective influence and persuasion rely on honesty and transparency. Real, genuine, positive persuasion makes no attempt to fool the audience, but rather gives a

The Benefits of Learning about this Skill

grouping of facts and information that the audience can consider to make the best choice. Learning the skill of effective influence using solid communication techniques can drastically improve self-esteem levels, job performance, and chances of securing positions of leadership.

Influence and persuasion should always be used for helping others, rather than hurting them. False information shouldn't be used or given, and if you have a good understanding of true ethical manipulation, it will never be necessary. There are many benefits to gain from learning about NLP, including an extreme increase in your persuasion abilities, which might be the most important social skill you could develop. Since NLP techniques are so valuable, that is what we'll be focusing on in much of this guide. This chapter was intended to illustrate how important this skill is, so hopefully you now have a fuller understanding of the subject.

Chapter 3:

Manipulation and Influence Techniques

The simplest and easiest method for manipulating others, particularly American citizens, is by appealing to their feelings. Although you can use logic to help people reach a logical decision, you can also guide them in feeling particular emotions that lead to the results you want. This is the essence of manipulation. This book will cover a wide variety of techniques to use for this, but first we are going to cover some tips that get you into the right frame of mind for persuading others. Here are some techniques and tips to help you along:

- **Get a Hold of your Own Feelings First:** It can be easier to influence or ethically manipulate someone who is more on the indecisive side, but you can also persuade people with a strong resolve to consider and come over to your point of view. Being aware of your own feelings and how they come across to others is an important part of this. In order to persuade others, you have to be relatable to them, and in order to be relatable, you have to know which emotions to show, how, and when.

- For example, accessing a confident state of mind when interacting with someone makes you come across as calm and collected, meaning that others, especially indecisive people, will gladly follow your lead. Exhibiting your adventurous or authoritative qualities can be especially influential when you're around someone who is more on the shy side. The key lies in knowing which personality traits to show and when and who to do that around.

- **Become Charismatic:** Throwing tantrums and crying to get your way might work for some, but being charismatic and having people like you is a much better way to exert influence and effectively manipulate the feelings others have of you. It's also a good way to reach for mutually beneficial outcomes to your persuasion. Charm is a foundational part of this. When you are likeable in the majority of situations, reacting with strong emotions in specific situations will have more impact on others. So study up on becoming more charismatic, dress well, and make sure you treat others with respect. All of that will help you be more influential.

- Being charismatic is all about getting people to feel comfortable around you. You can do this by showing that you care about them. Instead of simply talking about what you like and what you think, ask people for their input and opinions. This shows that you value them as a person and think they are worth listening to. In addition to this, make sure you make eye contact during conversations, but not too much. Essentially, you should be looking directly at someone's face for at least 60 percent of the conversation.

Manipulation

- **Humanize Yourself to Others:** One way to get others to trust you and open up to you more easily is to humanize yourself to them. One way to do this is to share personal information with them that is relevant and allows them to feel as though you trust them with something. When this happens, they are more likely to open up to you and allow you to influence them. This is similar to, and draws off of, the technique of reciprocation discussed in an earlier chapter of the book.

- People automatically like you more when you decide to confide something in them. Depending on the situation, this will vary, so use your judgment. For example if you are trying to persuade someone to trust your advice as a veterinarian, you could share a personal anecdote about having to put your lifelong companion, Fluffy, down when you were a kid, and how it all worked out for the best. If you wish for your friend to take your advice on a breakup, relate a story about a hard time you went through that is similar in nature.

- **Positivity:** When you are attempting to persuade or ethically manipulate another person, your worst enemy is doubt. You should maintain positive relations with the person you're talking to, and never resort to attacking or negativity. Not only does this poison possible relations between you and the other person, but it makes you a very ineffective influencer. Show your best qualities to make yourself relatable and likeable.

- **Mention Advantages and Benefits:** Getting people to come around to a specific way of thinking or acting often means you must display good reasons for them to do so. Mention explicit benefits and advantages to them coming around to your opinion on the matter. If you're trying to sell something to someone, for example, list the worries that they will be free from with your product.

There are many different ways to manipulate, control, and influence the feeling response that people have to you. Realizing this is the essence of leadership and true influence. Perhaps the most important skill of all is being a likeable person. Now that we have covered some of the benefits to manipulation (when used in a positive and uplifting manner), it's time to discuss some of the negative and harmful effects that irresponsible manipulation can lead to.

Chapter 4:

How to Recognize Negative Manipulation

One of the most important parts of learning about manipulation is figuring out how to protect yourself from it. Nearly everyone in this world has been manipulated negatively in some way or another, and it never feels good or nice. Everyone on this planet just wants to meet their own needs, but people who use negative manipulation use deceit and underhanded techniques for doing so, instead of honesty and an approach of mutual benefit. In essence, they don't care about your wants or needs, and only wish to serve themselves. This relies on subtly influencing another person with abusive, deceptive, or hidden tactics.

Veiled Hostility and Intimidation Tactics:

At first, it might come across as flattering, friendly, and harmless, like that person only has your best interests at heart, but that is never the case with negative manipulation. Sometimes, it's barely concealed hostility, and when someone uses these abusive techniques, they are trying to gain power over you. At times, you might not even know that you're being intimidated subconsciously. When you're used to manipulation from childhood or the past, it can be more difficult to recognize it or know what's happening because it's familiar and might even feel natural in some ways. You may feel an instinctual anger or discomfort, while the manipulator uses reasonable, ingratiating, or pleasant terms that appeal to your sympathy or guilt. This leads to you overriding your gut feelings and not knowing how to respond.

Who uses these Negative Tactics?

People in codependent relationships might have a hard time being assertive or direct, leading to the use of negative manipulation to achieve their personal goals. These types might also become victims of narcissists or sociopaths. Abusive partners might use these tactics, as well.

How to Recognize Negative Manipulation:

There are a few tactics that every manipulator uses, and these are favors and gifts, flattery, over the top apologies, fake sympathy, false concern, evasion techniques or avoidance, blackmail, making assumptions about you, playing with your mind, undermining your thoughts and feelings, bribing you, blaming you, faking innocence, making excuses, comparing, complaining, and guilt tripping. Let's look at a few of these techniques in detail:

- **Favors with "Strings Attached":** They will often utilize the technique of guilt either directly or in an implied way. They do you favors and then hold them over your head later when they want something from you.

- **Getting Power through Sympathy:** Some negative manipulators will deny agreements, conversations, or promises they made you. They might also intentionally start fights and then blame you in order to gain power by upsetting you.

Manipulation

- **Bribery:** Bribery is very commonly used by parents in order to get their kids to follow their instructions. For example, your parents might bribe you to go to the school they want you to attend, by buying you a new car.

- **Using Assumptions:** Negative manipulators will often make assumption aloud about you or your beliefs or intentions, and then respond to those assumptions. They will ignore what you say to the contrary as a way to justify their actions and feelings. They might even pretend as though you have agreed or decided something to effectively ignore your objections or input on the subject. For example, they will tell you how you feel, and respond to that, instead of asking you how you feel and listening.

- **Pressured Reciprocation:** We discussed the influence tactic of reciprocation, where you offer someone something small and then follow up with a larger request. This can be harmless, but when it's used with pressure or guilt, that's when it becomes a negative manipulation tactic. When you say no to their request, they will turn around and try to make themselves out to be the victim. It will be all about the manipulator and their personal issues, leading you to feel defensive.

- They will then bring up past occurrences of you not fulfilling their wishes, and lay a lot of blame on you to try to get you to agree with what they want. They don't care if it hurts you at all, in fact, as long as it makes you do what they want. You get the feeling, when it comes to a negative manipulator, that there are always hidden motives or strings attached when they offer something to you or act kind.

- **False Concern or Blackmail:** This is a tactic, which relies on "well-meaning worry", that is intended to make you doubt yourself or to invalidate your choices. The negative manipulator might also use shame, threats, intimidation, or anger tactics to get you to do what they want. They may shame you to make you feel doubt and insecurity, even masking this with a false compliment. People who use blackmail might also use anger to scare you, leading you to putting aside your wants and needs to do what they want.

- If this method doesn't work on you, they might switch suddenly to a more positive mood and act nice toward you. This could lead you to feel relieved and become willing to do what they ask you to do. They may also bring up shameful memories from your past and threaten to tell others about it if you don't comply with their wishes. This may lead the victim of the negative manipulation to feel fearful to say no. If they say no, they will likely experience insults from the manipulator, such as being called selfish.

- **Passive Aggressive Manipulation**: Some people, especially those who are on the shy side, use passive manipulation tactics, since most people with codependent personalities are not very assertive. They might act agreeable on the surface, telling people what they want to hear, and then break their agreements later on. Instead of responding honestly to an issue that could lead to fighting or some type of confrontation, they avoid instead, try to change the subject, or deny and blame, using rationalizations and excuses.

Manipulation

- They are afraid to be wrong, and due to finding it difficult to raise conflict, they say yes even when they don't agree, and then follow up with complaints or guilt trips about how hard it will be to accommodate the other person. When someone confronts them, they may feel shame and have a hard time claiming responsibility for their actions. So instead, they create excuses, blame others, or try to "fix" things by apologizing, even if they don't mean it.

- Even these passive tactics, which aren't as obvious as the tactics of anger or shaming, are a method for expressing hostile feelings. These could involve saying yes to a request and then "forgetting" to follow through on it, because you never wanted to in the first place.

- **Self-Pity and Criticism**: Negative manipulators might use flattery and charm, offering to do nice favors for you, help with something you need assistance with, or give you gifts in order to gain your love and acceptance. Then they will turn around and use manipulation tactics like self-pity, guilt, and criticism to get others to follow along with their desires. "Why are you always so selfish? I help you when you need it." They constantly pull the victim card.

The best way to figure out a defense against manipulation is to know who you're dealing with and going up against. Every negative manipulator has different tactics, and if they know you well, they're already aware of what triggers you. Become aware of their methods for doing this and learn to recognize it when they attempt to use them on you. Build up your self-respect and self-worth, which will be your greatest defense.

Chapter 5:

How to Avoid being Manipulated

Now that we have gone over some of the methods and tactics people use to negatively manipulate others, it's time to talk about how to avoid these methods. Negative manipulation can be defined as convincing others to do whatever you desire, without offering something of value back to them. How does this phenomenon work?

- **A Threat and no Value:** If a person says, "Help me finish this project or I'm going to be angry with you," they are trying to negatively manipulate your actions. They are not actually offering anything of value to you in return. However, if a friend offers you something of value in return for a favor, that isn't negative manipulation, because you're getting something back for the effort you put in.

- **Making another Responsible for their Emotions:** Another form of manipulation is telling someone that they are responsible for how you feel and that they should feel guilty for that. For example, telling them that if they don't come to your party, you will be highly disappointed. This implies that it's their fault how you feel. However, if you offer to introduce your friend to someone they have been wanting to meet at your party, you are offering a situation that allows both of you to win.

Why do People Manipulate?

What are people's reasons for manipulating others? These can be anything from innocent and even friendly reasons to mean and selfish, but for the sake of this chapter, we're going to focus on negative and selfish manipulation.

- **Misery Likes Company:** They do it because they gain satisfaction, on an emotional level, from seeing the frustrated or otherwise negative responses of others. Certain people are so unhappy with their lives and themselves that they try to bring others down by creating problems for them.

- **It makes them feel Powerful:** Someone who is insecure and feels powerless will often try to exert power in other areas to make up for it. Getting others to do what they want gives them temporary satisfaction.

- **A Lack of Importance:** Another reason why people negatively manipulate others is because they don't think that they are important. They believe that if they simply request what they wish for, they won't get it because they don't matter enough. So instead, they try to make us feel ashamed or guilty as a consequence for not doing what they want, as a preemptive measure from disappointment.

- **They are "too Good" for some Things:** Other negative manipulators simply think that they are too good for certain tasks. They might see other people as below them, and therefore expect those people to do the tasks that they don't want to do. This could be due to laziness, or simply an inflated sense of self.

- **Not Knowing how to get Things done:** Some negative manipulators don't think that they are capable of gaining what they want, and instead operate under the assumption that they must convince and pressure others to do their bidding for them.

- **Selfishly "Helping" Others:** Other negative manipulators actually convince themselves that what they are doing will help people. This is a common idea embraced by people who think that they know better than others what is best for everyone. Due to their beliefs that they have a higher intelligence or ability, they feel satisfied doing this, and convince themselves that the people being manipulated are better off for it.

Actually, the majority of negative manipulators are not actually bad people; they are simply misguided, inconsiderate, insensitive, selfish, and often times, weak and insecure. Some of them believe that the people they are manipulating are not as valuable as themselves, and that their desires and needs are not as important. This mistaken belief is what allows them to continue to act the way they do without considering the feelings of other people.

Different types of Negative Manipulation:

- **Turning your Emotions against you:** Techniques for manipulation vary widely, but usually, negative manipulators will attempt to get the feelings of others to work against them. They will try to do that by doing or saying things that are intended to stir up fear, anger, shame, guilt, or any other uncomfortable feeling. For example, they might insinuate that if we don't follow through on their suggestions or orders, something horrible will result.

- **Threats of Future Unpleasantness:** They might also try to describe to you all of the different types of unpleasant situations that could arise if you don't do what they want. They might imply or even overtly insist that something is our fault, responsibility, or duty, using ethics and morality to pressure us to come around to their ideas or demands. Some people will even throw every trick at us, warning us of the consequences of disappointing or letting them down.

- **Common Phrases Used:** They may imply to us that we will be so happy if we do what they want us to do, or that we will make them very happy, and that they will love us so much. They may also use phrases like "You need to…" or "You must…" or "You should…" as a way to subtly pressure you into following through on what they are asking of you. They will say those phrases and others which insinuate great consequences if you don't follow the obligation they are giving to you.

What do each of the above methods and techniques share in common with each other? The person doing the negative manipulation doesn't offer anything of value in return for fulfilling their wishes. Instead, the victim gets exploited by a created power imbalance.

How to Avoid being Negatively Manipulated by Others:

So, now that we have discussed some of the signs of negative manipulation, it's time to figure out how to avoid it and recognize when someone is trying to use it on you.

- **Be Aware of your Rights:** The absolute most important rule you can follow when dealing with someone who wants to manipulate you in negative ways is to know your own worth and rights. This way, you will always know when someone is attempting to violate them. So long as others are not getting harmed in the process, you should be defending yourself. Every human should have the right to have differing opinions from others, to protect yourself, to say "no" when you need to, and to decide what's important to you. You should also have the right of expressing your wants, opinions, and feelings, and always be treated with respect.

- Unfortunately, the world has plenty of people who won't want to acknowledge or respect your rights, especially negative manipulators. You will also come into contact with others who generally wish to take advantage at any opportunity. However, you can proudly defy this by letting them know that you are the one who runs your life, no one else.

- **Maintain Healthy Distance:** Another way to tell who is manipulative is to pay attention to the way someone acts in varying situations and in front of various individuals. Although everyone, to a degree, puts on different faces depending on where they are, most people who are harmfully manipulative are extreme about it. They might, for example, be extremely polite and friendly to one person, and completely disrespect another, or act like a victim one second, and then act controlling immediately after.

- If you notice someone acting this way regularly, it's a good sign to distance yourself from them and not engage with them unless it's an absolute necessity. Usually, the reasons behind these types of behavior are complicated, and it isn't your duty or responsibility to help or change that person. Trying to do so will often only lead to suffering on your part, so it's better not to expect much when you notice these signs.

- **Don't Blame yourself:** A person who wishes to manipulate others in harmful ways searches for weaknesses to exploit, so it makes sense that someone who has been victimized by one might blame themselves or feel inadequate. But in a situation like this, you should remember that it isn't you that's the issue here; you are being pressured to feel bad by someone else who is very good at making people feel bad.

- This is how they get their way. Instead, think about the relationship you have with this person and ask yourself if they are respecting you, demanding reasonable things of you, and whether you are both benefiting, or only one of you is. Ask yourself, also, if you feel good about yourself after spending time with this person, or if you would feel better being around them less. The way you answer these questions will lead to important answers about where the issue lies in the situation.

Manipulation

- **Questioning them:** Eventually, this type of person is going to demand or request things from you. Many times, these requests or others will take their needs into consideration, while completely ignoring yours. Next time you receive a solicitation that is completely unreasonable, turn the focus back to them by asking some questions. Ask them if their request is reasonable, or if what they are asking from you is fair. You can also try asking if you get to have an opinion in this matter, or ask what benefit you will be gaining from the arrangement.

- Each time you ask questions like this, you are holding a mirror up to them, allowing them to see what they are truly asking of you. If they are self-aware, they will likely retract their request or demand. But there may be some cases, such as dealing with a narcissist, who will keep insisting without even considering your questions. If that happens, follow these guidelines.

- **Don't Answer Immediately:** One way to combat manipulation is to use time as a resource. Often, the manipulator will not only ask you to fulfill an unreasonable demand, but they will want an answer immediately. When this happens, rather than answering right away, use time and distance yourself from their request and influence. This can be done by telling them that you will think about it. Although these words are simple, they give your power back to you, giving you the option to weigh the advantages and disadvantages of the situation and let you work out something better, if need be.

- **Teach yourself to say "No" when needed:** Saying "no" is difficult for many people, since we are often taught and conditioned to be polite whenever possible. Being able to confidently but politely say "no" comes with learning communication skills. When this is articulated effectively, you can hold onto your self-respect, and also continue a healthy relationship. Keep in mind that your personal rights include deciding what matters to you, being able to turn down a request free from guilt, and choosing health and happiness for yourself. You are responsible for your life, not the person who is making unreasonable demands of you.

- **Create a Consequence:** Next time a negative manipulator tries to violate your rights, and refuses to accept your answer, set a consequence for their behavior. Knowing how to assert and identify appropriate consequences is a crucial skill for standing down someone who is being very difficult or disrespectful. If you can articulate this clearly and thoroughly, your consequences will cause them to pause and stop violating you, shifting to a position of respect.

How to Confront a Bully in a Safe Way:

Not all manipulators resort to bullying, but many of them do. Someone is being a bully when they use intimidation or harm to get what they want from you. Remember, always, that a bully chooses people they see as weak to pick on, and compliance and passivity will only strengthen this. However, a lot of bullies are afraid and insecure deep down, so when their victim starts to stand up for themselves, this will often lead the bully to back off. Whether this situation is occurring in a playground or at the office, it applies, most of the time. Keep in mind that many bullies have actually withstood bullying and violence. Although this doesn't excuse their behaviors, it does help the victim to understand.

Chapter 6:

A Guide to Positive Manipulation (Persuasion)

Leadership and manipulation go together, but there is a distinct difference between the type of manipulation discussed in the last chapter, and ethical (or positive) manipulation. Positive manipulation relies on using personal influence to gain a response or outcome. To put it another way, it relies on convincing someone to do what you are asking. This definition makes it easy to understand why the most powerful leaders in the world are often very skilled at ethical manipulation. Regardless of its negative connotations, manipulation is not always a bad thing. Actually, countless leaders in business could enjoy advantages from using some of these methods in their set of skills. One of these skills is using manipulation in a responsible, ethical, and positive way.

What makes Positive Manipulation Ethical?

Positive, ethical manipulation methods have outcomes and goals that have been thoroughly defined, and are always motivated by goal-seeking and accomplishment. It's not appropriate at all to try to manipulate people for pleasure or your own personal achievement, while disregarding their rights or desires. But it is necessary and appropriate to use this

A Guide to Positive Manipulation (Persuasion)

tactic as a way to help people achieve shared visions and to further an organization or business.

What to use Positive Manipulation Methods for:

Influence and persuasion skills are extremely useful and powerful for many different reasons. They can be used to convince a child to follow through on something, to change ideas in a county or community, or to help change the minds or actions of employees and customers at work. When you decide to develop these skills and methods, you instantly increase your own personal influence, leadership abilities, and power.

- **Influence:** Ethical manipulation mainly relies on persuading or influencing others to follow through on something they wouldn't do on their own. This could be thoughts or actions, and although the person might naturally choose something else, a leader who ethically manipulates them exerts subtle and appropriate pressure in order to help that person reach an outcome that is most desired.

- **Persuasion:** Subordinates and leaders often disagree on objectives, processes, and concepts, and this is entirely natural. But using techniques that rely on positive and ethical manipulation can help persuade peers or subordinates to come over to the way you think of things. Instead, of overtly pressuring, bullying, or bulldozing, these methods allow you to share your ideas and give them a chance to agree with you or shift to your perspective.

Manipulation

- **Inspiration:** When someone uses manipulation and has the correct motivation behind it, it can actually be very inspiring to the people involved. If, for example, you're looking at a difficult, long project, you can give the team some easy simple projects now in order to help them feel more capable and confident. This is, technically, manipulation, but it's for a good cause and helps the people involved. Manipulation is all about getting people to feel or act in certain ways. For example, getting people to be enthusiastic and exciting about something they are doing.

- **Unity:** Conflicts at work and home are a natural part of social interaction. But it's perfectly possible to manipulate a situation in order to bring about more unity. This relies on recognizing that a conflict is about to happen and finding ways to manipulate the situation to prevent problems. This is a great example of manipulation being a positive, rather than negative, influence. People who can do this are often seen as valuable assets to group situations or work environments, because they know how to mediate and keep the peace. These are valuable abilities to have.

- **For Defending yourself:** There are many benefits to learning about persuasion. Not only is it useful for using it yourself to get things done, but you can use it to protect yourself from manipulation that isn't good for you. For example, perhaps a friend is pressuring you to go out and drink all night when you have to be to work the next morning, just because they don't have to work. Being aware of persuasion tactics will help you to recognize theirs and persuade them to drop the subject.

A Guide to Positive Manipulation (Persuasion)

You can also use these tactics to exert your own will and rights in difficult situations.

- You can study your surroundings and the people around you in order to find the correct methods for getting done what you need to do. This can be at work, at home, or in your personal friendships and romantic relationships.

Why Compliance Manipulation is Ineffective:

In this section of the book, we're going to consider some main techniques for persuasion that can be used in nearly any situation. But before getting into these methods, we should go over what persuasion means to have a fuller understanding of it. This is crucial to be aware of, since persuasion can often be confused with pressuring others into compliance. The latter is often focused only on changing the behaviors of other people, while persuasion tactics try to get people or groups or people to feel and think positively about the thoughts or actions you wish for them to have.

- **Manipulation for Compliance:** There are lots of ways to manipulate people into complying with your ideas. Some examples of this include threats of legal action if you don't follow laws (like a ticket for not wearing your seatbelt), or a parent threatening their child with punishment for not finishing their homework or cleaning up their room. These are distinctly different from typical techniques for persuasion, because a change of feelings or beliefs is not necessary for the people to act or change their behaviors. They only have to be able to feel the fear and recognize it to comply.

- **Resentment and a Lack of Motivation:** The problem with techniques like the ones listed above is that without the fear or threat, people wouldn't follow through on what they're being asked to do. In addition to this, nobody enjoys being negatively manipulated, meaning that they are more likely to feel resentful of these tactics once they realize what is happening to them. Sadly, this form of manipulation is still very common, but although it can work for some cases, it's not a very sophisticated or effective tool.

When you look back at being manipulated into compliance, either by authority figures at school, bosses at work, or your own parents in childhood, it usually isn't a very good feeling. More often than not, it leads to negative feelings and interactions, and this is because it's based on fear, instead of free will and choice. The question then becomes, how is it possible to get people to do what you want them to do of their own volition? They must make the choice themselves if they are going to continue to choose it.

Using NLP and Creating Agreement for Successful Positive Manipulation:

The trick here is to use agreement to be successful at positive manipulation and persuasion. You have to create a few different levels of agreement, such as spiritual, emotional, mental, and physical. Consider an individual getting carried on by a strong current of water, such as a river. You have to construct a strong enough agreement stream that it pulls the person in your direction. How is this possible to do?

- **Connect:** Studies done in hypnosis and NLP show that establishing rapport with someone else makes them much more agreeable to your ideas, suggestions, and actions. This can be done by subtly mirroring them, as mentioned earlier in the book. Don't think of it as imitating or mocking, but rather as complementing the other person's facial expressions and gestures. This gives them more positive feelings towards you and makes them more suggestible to your ideas.

- If you practice this often and truly understanding the concepts behind establishing connection and rapport with others, you can utilize mirroring and matching as a technique to bring others into positive alignment with yourself. Furthermore, this can be done in such a way that the other individual has no idea that you're using a technique at all. That's because this is a subliminal method that everyone responds to in spite of themselves. This leads to a nice, warm, harmonious sense that the two of you are relating to each other.

- **Trust:** Not many people are aware of the way that nonverbal communication happens between two people, even though this is where the majority of signals are being sent. When you mirror and match someone else's mannerisms and expressions, their subconscious is receiving a message that it's okay to trust you and let their guard down. This is because you are acting like them, and most humans relate easier to people that they see as similar to them. Even if the person doesn't know why on a conscious level, they will feel more comfortable with you.

- Trust is necessary for getting someone to come around to your ideas or goals. It's true that you can pressure someone into going along with what you want, but if there is any chance that they will enjoy it and do it willingly, you have to create rapport and positive feelings in your interactions. Only then is persuasion or ethical manipulation possible.

- **Breaking Patterns:** In addition to mirroring to build rapport, other NLP techniques exist for strong subliminal influence. One example of this is using questions in order to re-direct someone's attention or focus to something else, or to break mental patterns. Questions are effective because they are hard to resist answering. Our minds automatically want to try to solve questions as soon as they are asked. For example, if someone asks you what good things have happened in your life lately, your state of mind automatically begins focusing on positivity.

- **Storytelling and Metaphors:** Another method for persuading others is using storytelling and metaphors to get your point or idea across to them. People who specialize in persuasion can make this tactic very complicated, but it's actually effective right away, in a lot of cases. This can be done by sharing a story that shows you reaching a conclusion that you are hoping they will also reach, using positive descriptive terms. Make sure you are making something sound highly positive, if you want someone to agree with you.

- **Set a Goal:** If you have any desires to accomplish something specific, you have to get specific about defining it. It's too easy to meander through interactions and daily life without having a clear cut vision of what you wish to do. In order to effectively persuade and ethically manipulate others, set a desired goal for the interaction you have with them. This could be to simply call or text them, send a letter in the mail, set up a meeting, or convince them to sign up for something. Decide ahead of time what the action or outcome will be that you wish for the individual to come around to.

- **Get Confident and Passionate:** Become enthusiastic about your service, product, idea, or concept. Enthusiasm is contagious and effective for persuasion. Think about it, when you're talking to someone who is trying to convince you about something, is it easier to listen to them when they are droning on and seem bored out of their minds, or when they seem completely sold on and excited about the idea? It's important to get excited. This can be done by emotionally connecting with whatever advantages and benefits you are providing with your idea. Think about who the idea has helped and will help.

- In addition to this, giving logical perspectives is also helpful when it comes to ethical manipulation and persuading people. Keep in mind that people often make their choices based on emotion, and later justify those choices using logical reasons. Appealing to both of these is your best bet.

- **Be Upfront and Ask Directly:** Another technique is to simply ask directly for whatever it is that you want. This might mean a date, asking someone to buy your product, or convincing them to sign up for something. If you don't ask, you will never know! A lot of times, people simply don't know what to do, and offering an action, idea, or solution can be helpful for everyone involved.

Manipulation

Practice all of the skills listed above to help your influence and persuasion skills develop and grow into strong abilities. Becoming great with persuasion and ethical manipulation relies first on understanding the foundations of persuasion, and then using techniques to support them. Keep in mind that as long as you are offering something of value in return for what you are asking of someone, you are using persuasion and influence in a positive way. Being aware of what persuasion and manipulation tactics look like can also help protect you against people trying to use them adversely against you.

Conclusion

Thank you again for downloading this book!

I hope this book was able to help you to understand how prevalent and important the subject of manipulation is in our everyday lives. Although the word "manipulation" typically has a negative connotation, it isn't always that way. We encounter this phenomenon far more often than we consciously realize, and living the most advantageous life possible means getting in touch with this and using it to your benefit.

With the information in this book, you will never again be taken advantage of by manipulative people without your best interests at heart. In addition to this, you can utilize methods of positive and ethical manipulation to influence and lead others in beneficial ways. When you understand this tool of social power and influence, you can achieve whatever it is you wish to achieve in life. Our worlds are increasingly connected and social, so this is an invaluable skill to develop. Luckily, it can be learned and constantly improved, like any other skill in life.

Finally, if you enjoyed this book, then I'd like to ask you for a favor, would you be kind enough to leave a review for this book? It'd be greatly appreciated!

www.ingramcontent.com/pod-product-compliance
Lightning Source LLC
Chambersburg PA
CBHW052106110526
44591CB00013B/2376